# HAVE YOURSELF A
# MERRY
# LITTLE
# COCKTAIL

For Disco, who got us to five o'clock

# HAVE YOURSELF A
# MERRY LITTLE COCKTAIL

80 cheerful tipples to warm up winter

## Emma Stokes

POP PRESS

# CONTENTS

# A VERY MERRY INTRODUCTION

*'Twas the night before Christmas, when came an idea to start merrily stirring cocktails full of cheer*

*And drink them together by the chimney place fire – but what tipples would fill us with festive desire?*

*The people were restless with dreams of libations, so they reached for a book full of such inspirations*

*And at once they exclaimed with such jolly delight; 'Merry little cocktails to all, and to all a good night!'*

Have you ever been stuck at home over the holidays, looked at the time, and it has been *exactly* cocktail o'clock? Then *Have Yourself a Merry Little Cocktail* is the perfect companion for you.

This book contains tried and tested recipes that are guaranteed to add some cheer and impress your friends and family alike. There are presents for Christmas, warmers for Winter, brews for Bonfires – everything from Halloween to Valentine's Day has a tipple just waiting to be made. And as an extra stocking filler, there are non-alcoholic and low-alcoholic variants for many of the recipes – look out for the ❄ symbol.

There are also guides on equipment, glassware, garnishes and essential ingredients for your cupboard, making this book a one-stop-shop (excluding your Christmas shopping) for all your merry needs.

And what would a festive book be, if not a little bit over the top, pun-ladened and guaranteed to convert even the biggest Scrooge?

So, get shaking and stirring, and remember – it doesn't matter if you've been naughty or nice; it's always five o'clock somewhere!

Emma

@ginmonkeyuk

# COCKTAIL CHEAT SHEET

# BARTENDER'S KIT

*The kit below is the standard bartending gear you'll use to make these recipes. Most of them you can pick up pretty easily and you'll feel more of a festive mixologist if you've got them, but I've listed alternatives where possible.*

### Bar spoon

For measuring or pouring, you could also use a teaspoon (a standard 5ml teaspoon is generally the right size).

For stirring, the term mixing 'spoon' can be misleading as what you need is something to help move the ingredients and ice around in the mixing glass. Something long and thin like a chopstick or knife that can fit around the ice is much better than a tablespoon with a large head.

### Cocktail shaker

An essential purchase, although anything that is watertight that allows the ice to be rapidly moved in and around the liquid will also work. A sports flask or protein shaker are often touted as good substitutes. In my experience jam jars are a little small, but larger sauce jars could work.

### Measuring jigger

You could use any kitchen utensil used for measuring, providing you're able to be accurate. For some cocktails with simple ingredients and measurements you can convert into parts (so for a negroni 25ml becomes 1 part) and you can then use an egg cup to measure (so one part gin, one part Campari and one part sweet vermouth). Just be aware you might end up with a much larger finished cocktail!

### Mixing glass

You could use any large receptacle that can hold a reasonable amount of ice and will allow you to stir.

### Strainer and fine strainer

Believe it or not, but a whisk placed inside a cocktail shaker can provide a decent enough strainer to catch large pieces of ice (the main purpose of a simple strainer).

Fine strainers are designed to catch any pulp from ingredients and small pieces of ice, so a sieve is the best substitute. Just be careful to pour slowly into the middle of the glass under the sieve. A friend to hold the sieve is very welcome!

# COCKTAIL ESSENTIALS

**The recipes in this book use all sorts of spirits, liqueurs, mixers, juices and garnishes. Some of them you'll definitely have around the house, some will be easy to pick up, and others will take a little more planning to get your hands on. I've listed what I consider the essentials in each category.**

### Key spirits

- Gin
- Rum – gold rum will work for most of the rum recipes
- Brandy
- Vodka
- Scotch whisky

### Liqueurs and other spirits

- Triple sec
- Creme de cacao
- Apple brandy, or Calvados
- Cherry or berry liqueur
- Dry and sweet vermouths

### Non-alcoholic spirits and replacements

*Non-alcoholic spirits brands have really upped their game, so it's worth investing in a couple of replacements for your favourite spirits, if you're going down the alcohol-free route.*

- Non-alcoholic botanical spirit (replacement for gin and other white spirits)
- Non-alcoholic aromatic or grain spirit (replacement for whiskies and some cognacs)
- Non-alcoholic sparkling wine

- Almond extract
- Vanilla extract

## Mixers

- Champagne
- Espresso
- Ginger beer
- Milk – or your preferred milk substitute

## Syrups

- Sugar syrup *(1:1)* – equal parts caster sugar and water, stirred together until dissolved
- Gingerbread syrup

## Fruit juices

*Where possible, use freshly squeezed juice for the brightest tasting drinks.*

- Lemon juice
- Lime juice
- Orange juice
- Cranberry juice
- Apple juice – preferably cloudy apple juice

## Garnishes and other ingredients

- Lemon, limes, oranges
- Nutmeg
- Cinnamon – ground and cinnamon sticks
- Cream – single and double
- Eggs – free-range and organic where possible
- Maraschino cherries

# GLASSWARE

· · · · · · · · · · · · · · · · · · · · · · · · · · · · · · · · · · · ·

*The glasses listed below are all used throughout this book. I've listed some household alternatives where possible, but just like the wrapping on a Christmas gift – presentation is important.*

### Champagne flute

A glass for special occasions; you'll need these for a good festive toast.

### Coffee or tea mugs

Everyone has one too many of these in their cupboards.

### Copa de Balon glass

A glass for a gin and tonic; you could use a large wine glass in its place.

### Coupe glass

The essential, go-to cocktail glass for drinks without ice.

### Highball or collins glass

These tall, thin glasses are for 'tall' mixed cocktails with lots of ice; a collins glass is usually taller and narrower.

### Hurricane glass

A specific glass for drinks like coladas and slings; you could use a highball glass in its place.

### Martini glass

The formal glass for a martini; you could use a coupe glass instead.

### Old Fashioned glass

Otherwise known as a rocks glass; any short, wide glass will do.

### Toddy glass

Otherwise known as a hot toddy glass or Irish coffee glass, these are for hot drinks; you could use a coffee or tea mug in its place.

### Wine glass

Mostly for wine, sometimes for sangria or gin and tonics; you've probably broken a few of these doing the washing up after a party.

# GLOSSARY

● ● ● ● ● ● ● ● ● ● ● ● ● ● ● ● ● ● ● ● ● ● ● ● ● ● ● ● ● ● ● ● ● ● ● ● ●

*Here are some of the more technical bartending and mixing terms used throughout this book. Don't strain yourself too hard though – I've floated the explanations of them below.*

### Churn with a bar spoon

Used where you have solid ingredients like herbs alongside liquid ones. It's also used where a drink features crushed ice (like a mojito) to ensure consistency through the drink. Slide the spoon down the side of the glass and lift the ingredients through to combine.

### Float

The bowl of a spoon can be used to float one ingredient on top of another. Place the tip of the spoon bowl at the top of the layer you want to float something on and slowly pour the liquid on to the bowl of the spoon, slowly moving the spoon up as the liquid floats.

### Muddle

A term used to describe pressing or squishing ingredients. Often used for berries prior to shaking to ensure the berry is easily incorporated into the drink without needing a very hard shake motion, or for herbs to release their oils into a cocktail.

### Rim the glass and dip

Some cocktails feature a flavoured rim (the most famous is probably a salt rim on a margarita). To achieve this you need something dry (sugar, salt, etc.) and something wet to help it stick. Citrus juice will suffice for some, but for heavier ingredients like edible glitter you'll need something stickier like sugar syrup.

### Strain/fine strain

Straining describes pouring a cocktail out of a shaker through something that catches the large pieces of ice to stop them ending up in the final drink. Fine straining is usually combined with straining and refers to the use of a tea strainer or similar to catch any smaller pieces of ice, or large pieces of fresh ingredients (such as berry pips) from ending up in your glass to give a smoother texture.

### To top/top with

To add something to lengthen your drink after you've shaken, stirred or built your cocktail. Like adding tonic to a G&T, you should pour until the final cocktail is around 1cm from the top of your chosen glass to ensure you can carry it without spilling it!

# THE COCKTAILS OF CHRISTMAS PRESENT

# SPICE AND SLOE

●●●●●●●●●●●●●●●●●●●●●●●●●●●●●●●●●●●●●●

**Spices and berries are traditional signs that Christmas season has finally arrived**

Does anything scream Christmas more than spice and berries? This cocktail has hints of stewed berries, forest floor, toasty cinnamon and a bit of Bakewell tart too. Spice and Sloe is a drink for those rare, sunny afternoons over the Christmas break.

**Serves** 1 • **Method** Mix • **Glassware**

*Cloudy apple juice*
*Hayman's Spiced Sloe Gin*

Fill an Old Fashioned glass with ice. Add cloudy apple juice, leaving room at the top for the gin. Use a spoon to float the gin on top.

You could also drink this as a warm cocktail – add the cloudy apple juice to a saucepan and put over a medium heat. Heat until the juice is warm (but not boiling) and take off the heat. Pour the juice into a coffee mug and add the gin.

If you can't get your hands on a bottle of Hayman's brilliantly seasonal spiced sloe gin, you could use a normal sloe gin instead.

# THE LITTLE DONKEY

*Little Donkey, Little Donkey, love your ginger way*

Sometimes, with all the radiators on and relatives in every room, Christmas afternoons can get a little too warm. The Little Donkey combines the flavours of Christmas and the kick of ginger beer to provide a moment of refreshing respite.

**Serves** 1  •  **Method** Shake  •  **Glassware**

*50ml vodka*
*10ml (2 teaspoons) lime juice*
*5ml (1 teaspoon) gingerbread syrup*
*Ginger beer, to top*

**Garnish** Sprig of mint, a 'horse's neck' of lime peel

Fill a cocktail shaker with ice. Add the vodka, lime juice and gingerbread syrup and shake until cold. Strain into Old Fashioned glass filled with ice. Top with ginger beer and add a sprig of mint.

To make the horse's neck garnish, take a vegetable peeler and carefully remove as much of the peel from a lime as possible in one long piece. Place into your glass before the ice, curling it around the edges of the glass.

For an extra kick, you could add a dash or two of hot sauce to the shaker, before shaking.

# ST CLEMENT'S 75

*Oranges and lemons, say the bells of St Clement's*

The St Clement's 75 is a Christmassy twist on the classic French 75. It incorporates the citrus from the classic nursery rhyme 'Oranges and Lemons' in the form of a spiced orange syrup, creating a cocktail perfect for Christmas morning and the opening of presents.

**Serves** 1 • **Method** Shake • **Glassware**

**For the cocktail**
*50ml London dry gin*
*25ml lemon juice*
*25ml spiced orange syrup*
*(see opposite)*
*Champagne/prosecco, to top*

**For the spiced orange syrup**
*6–8 oranges*
*2 whole star anise*
*10–12 whole cloves*
*5–10 slices of fresh ginger*
*½ vanilla pod*
*Caster sugar*

To make the spiced orange syrup, juice the oranges into a pan and then add the star anise, cloves, ginger and vanilla pod. Place over a medium heat until it starts to bubble. Remove from the heat and leave to infuse for 30 minutes. Strain into a measuring jug, add an equal volume of caster sugar and mix. This method makes about 500ml syrup – enough for 20 cocktails. It will keep in the fridge in a sterilised, sealed bottle or jar for up to a week, if not all used immediately.

To make the cocktail, fill a cocktail shaker with ice and add the gin, lemon juice and 25ml of the prepared syrup. Shake until cold. Strain into a champagne flute and top with champagne or prosecco.

### ❄ *Make it a St Clements 86*
*Swap the gin for a non-alcoholic botanical spirit like Seedlip and top with soda water.*

# LET IT SLOE

* * * * * * * * * * * * * * * * * * * * * * * * * * * * * * * * * *

**When everything is said and done, let it pun, let it pun, let it pun**

A wonderful balance of sweet, dry and crisp, the Let it Sloe combines classic Christmas flavours with a classic Christmas pun. There is no better time to drink this tipple, than when opening some crackers, popping on paper hats, and getting everyone chuckling with a bad joke.

Serves 1 • Method Stir • Glassware

*30ml sloe gin*
*15ml port*
*10ml (2 teaspoons) apricot brandy*
*2 dashes of Angostura bitters*
*Tonic water, to top*

Fill an Old Fashioned glass with ice. Add the gin, port, brandy and bitters. Top with tonic and stir.

# SLOE GINGER

. . . . . . . . . . . . . . . . . . . . . . . . . . . . . . . . . . . .

### *Put some ginger in to balance out the gin*

When Christmas gives you sloe gin, top it up with some ginger
beer. Simple, elegant, bright and warm, the Sloe GINger is
perfect for any time in the holiday period when you feel like
adding a bit of fizzy kick to the mix.

**Serves** 1  •  **Method** Stir  •  **Glassware**

*50ml sloe gin*
*1 orange wedge*
*Ginger beer, to top*

**Garnish** *Orange slice*

Fill a highball glass with ice. Add the sloe gin. Squeeze the
orange wedge into the drink and then discard the orange. Top
with the ginger beer, stir and add an orange slice to finish.

### ❄ *Make it a No GINger*
*Replace the sloe gin with 30ml of this festive cranberry and orange*
*spiced syrup: add 300ml orange juice, 100g demerara sugar,*
*3 cinnamon sticks, 5 cloves, zest of 1 orange and 6 tablespoons*
*cranberry sauce to a pan, and warm over a medium heat. Stir*
*until dissolved, remove from the heat and leave to infuse for*
*15 minutes, then strain through a sieve. This makes about 350ml syrup*
*– enough for 11–12 cocktails – so keep in the fridge in a sterilised,*
*sealed bottle or jar for up to a week, if not using immediately.*

# CHERRY SOUR

• • • • • • • • • • • • • • • • • • • • • • • • • • • • • • • • • • • •

*Tastes so good at a late-night hour, sweet and delectable Cherry Sour*

Like Christmas dinner and cranberry sauce, cherries and bourbon are good bedfellows. The notes from the cherry marry excellently with the oak notes of the bourbon, and the addition of the lemon juice adds balance and lift. Just make sure there's enough to go around, or you'll look quite the turkey.

**Serves** 1 • **Method** Shake • **Glassware**

*20ml bourbon whiskey*
*20ml cherry liqueur*
*30ml lemon juice*

*15ml sugar syrup*
*15ml egg white*
*1 dash of Angostura bitters*

**Garnish** *Orange wedge and maraschino cherry*

Fill a cocktail shaker with ice. Place all the ingredients into the shaker and shake until cold. Strain into an Old Fashioned glass filled with ice. Garnish with an orange wedge and a maraschino cherry on top.

### ❄ *Make it a Cherry Red-NOsed Sour*

*Replace the bourbon whiskey with a mixture of 15ml water and 5ml vanilla extract. Replace the cherry liqueur with a cherry syrup or 3 tablespoons of cherry jam. The dash of Angostura bitters is not alcoholic enough to classify the drink as alcoholic, but you can leave it out if you prefer.*

# CHRISTMAS CAKE MANHATTAN

*This is a festive Manhattan to make when you're full from dinner and can't eat your cake*

This tipple is as Christmassy as a Manhattan is going to get – the classic flavours of a Christmas cake, distilled down into a guilt-free drink. Well, maybe not guilt-free, but certainly less guilt, anyway. Perfect for having your cake and drinking it too.

**Serves** 1 • **Method** Stir • **Glassware**

*50ml bourbon whiskey*
*5ml (1 teaspoon) orgeat*
*5ml (1 teaspoon) cherry liqueur*
*5ml (1 teaspoon) cognac*

**Garnish** *Maraschino cherry, dusted with cinnamon*

Fill a mixing glass with ice. Add all the ingredients and stir until cold. Strain into a chilled martini glass.

Take a maraschino cherry out of its syrup, place on a plate and dust with ground cinnamon. (If you're using fresh cherries, dip in some sugar syrup first to make sure the cinnamon sticks.) Make a small incision in the bottom of the cherry with a knife and place the cherry on the rim of the glass.

# SHERRY CHRISTMAS SOUR

- - - - - - - - - - - - - - - - - - - - - - - - - - - - - - - - - - -

**We wish you a merry Christmas, we wish you a sherry Christmas, and a fortified year**

In this tipple, the big, festive flavour of sherry is brightened by the lemon juice and rounded by the egg white. A Sherry Christmas Sour is a drink best for the outside, whether that's a cold walk around the garden, or a southern-hemisphere stand-and-chat by the barbecue.

Serves 1 • **Method** Shake • **Glassware**

*60ml sherry*
*20ml lemon juice*
*15ml sugar syrup*
*1 egg white*

Fill a cocktail shaker with ice Place all the ingredients into the shaker and shake until cold Fine strain into a chilled coupe glass.

Depending on what type of sherry you use, the character of the drink will change. Using a dry sherry like a fino or Manzanilla will give the drink notes of fresh green fruit, while using an oloroso will give it a deeper, nuttier flavour.

# CHRISTMAS ESPRESSO MARTINI

*Everyone loves an espresso martini – even dressed in fun sweaters and Christmas-themed beanies*

Who doesn't love an espresso martini? Well, this one you can make at home over the holidays, so no one has to see you choosing this delicacy over something supposedly more 'chic'. The addition of the gingerbread syrup makes it perfect for a Christmas lunch digestif.

**Serves** 1 • **Method** Shake • **Glassware**

*50ml vodka*
*25ml espresso coffee, chilled*
*15ml gingerbread syrup*

**Garnish** *Gingerbread syrup, ground cinnamon, 3 coffee beans*

Rim a chilled martini glass with some gingerbread syrup, dip in cinnamon and set aside.

Fill a cocktail shaker with ice. Add all the ingredients and shake until cold. Strain into the prepared martini glass and add the coffee beans on top.

### ❄ Make it a Christmas EspressNO Martini
*Swap the vodka for a non-alcoholic spirit.*

### ❄ Make it an Christmas EspressNO
*Take out the vodka entirely and serve in an espresso cup with a whipped cream float.*

# RHUBARB AND GINGER NEGRONI

*Children will wish for a toy or a pony, but adults who are nice get a rhubarb negroni*

This is a negroni for those who love Christmas. Kicking off your Christmas drinks with a festively tweaked tipple will set a fun and festive mood, and impress veteran and amateur drink enthusiasts alike.

**Serves** 1 • **Method** Stir • **Glassware**

*40ml rhubarb-styled, or rhubarb and ginger-styled gin*
*20ml sweet vermouth*
*20ml Campari*
*3.5ml (½ teaspoon) gingerbread syrup*

**Garnish** Orange slice

Fill an Old Fashioned glass with ice. Add all the ingredients and stir, then garnish with the orange slice.

If you can't get your hands on any rhubarb-styled gin, you could just use a London dry gin instead. If that's the case, increase the quantity of gingerbread syrup to 5ml (1 teaspoon).

# PEPPERMINTINI

●●●●●●●●●●●●●●●●●●●●●●●●●●●●●●●●●●●●●●●●●

***The prettiest sight to see is a peppermint martini in your own two hands***

In the days after Christmas, there's always leftover candy and cream lying about. Put them to good use in this delicious Peppermintini – perfect for those sugar cravings we get when we're 'meant to be starting that diet'. The diet can wait, but the candy won't last much longer.

**Serves** 1  ●  **Method** Shake  ●  **Glassware**

*5ml (1 teaspoon) green peppermint liqueur (or use a white liqueur with a drop of green food colouring)*
*40ml vodka*
*15ml peppermint white liqueur*
*40ml creme de cacao white*
*30ml double cream*

**Garnish** *A mini candy cane*

Add the 5ml green peppermint liqueur to a chilled martini glass and set aside.

Fill a cocktail shaker with ice. Add the remaining ingredients and shake until cold. Slowly strain into the prepared martini glass, so that the green liqueur remains largely at the bottom of the glass. Garnish by hanging a mini candy cane over the rim.

# RUDOLPH THE RED-NOSED COLLINS

*Rudolph with your taste so bright, won't you be my drink tonight?*

The Rudolph the Red-nosed Collins is a fun drink, and the perfect accompaniment to opening presents or toasting a Christmas meal. Make sure to include the garnish with this one – the holly represents a reindeer's antlers, and the cherry is for the most famous reindeer of them all, Rudolph.

**Serves** 1 • **Method** Shake • **Glassware**

*60ml pink gin (try to use one without a high sugar content)*
*30ml lemon juice*
*15ml sugar syrup*
*2 slices of fresh ginger*
*Soda water, to top*

**Garnish** *Sprig of holly, maraschino cherry*

Muddle the ginger in the bottom of a cocktail shaker and fill with ice. Add the gin, lemon juice and the sugar syrup and shake until cold. Strain into a highball glass and top with soda water.

Add a maraschino cherry and a sprig of holly to the glass. If you're feeling adventurous you could try and poke two holly leaves through the top of the cherry to create antlers.

You could also be a little fancier and replace the soda water with prosecco or Champagne; if this is the case, fine strain into a Champagne flute instead.

## ❄️ *Make it a Rudolph the Red-NOsed Collins*

*Leave out the gin entirely. Swap the sugar syrup for a juniper syrup, increasing the volume to 20ml. Swap the soda water for a cream soda – a sweeter soda is needed to balance the lemon juice.*

# NEGRONI FIZZ

**If the festive season is becoming chronic, a negroni fizz could be just the tonic**

Part negroni and part gin fizz, this drink might have a bit of an identity crisis but will still please those who love either or both of those classic tipples. The bubbles bring life to the staunch flavours of Campari and vermouth; an ideal drink to refresh the mood if things are getting a little stale in those post-Christmas days.

**Serves** 1 • **Method** Shake • **Glass**

*25ml gin*
*20ml Campari*
*25ml sweet vermouth*
*Champagne, to top*

**Garnish** *A quartered slice of orange*

Fill a cocktail shaker with ice. Add the gin, Campari and sweet vermouth and shake until cold. Strain into a champagne glass, filling it to about half full. Top with champagne and put a quartered slice of orange on the rim of the glass.

You could use prosecco or sparkling wine in place of the champagne, or, if you're feeling experimental, you could use tonic and serve it in a highball glass instead. Using flavoured tonics, like a pink peppercorn tonic, will spice up the recipe, while a Mediterranean-style tonic will give it a herbal edge.

# GINGER MARGARITA

**Christmas isn't always cold and grey, so drink this on a sunny Christmas day**

Whether it's just getting too stuffy indoors, or your Christmas is one of summer and sunnier shores, sometimes the day calls for a refreshing margarita. This Ginger Margarita is perfect for any moment when you just need to cool down.

**Serves** 1 • **Method** Shake • **Glassware**

50ml tequila reposado
25ml ginger syrup
10ml (2 teaspoons) ginger liqueur
25ml lime juice

**Garnish** *Slice of lime*

Fill a cocktail shaker with ice. Add all the ingredients and shake until cold.

Strain into an Old Fashioned glass filled with ice and add a slice of lime.

# WHITE CHRISTMAS COLADA

*May all your piña coladas be white*

Inspired by the classic piña colada, this quick and simple coconut delight adds a bit of holiday sweetness with the creme de cacao and vanilla. A perfect drink for getting caught in the rain, or if you're feeling thirsty around midnight.

**Serves** 1 • **Method** Shake • **Glassware**

*45ml gold rum*
*20ml coconut rum*
*10ml (2 teaspoons) creme de cacao white*
*45ml unsweetened coconut milk*
*5ml (1 teaspoon) lime juice*
*3 drops of vanilla extract*

**Garnish** *Dusting of cocoa powder*

Fill a cocktail shaker with ice. Add all the ingredients and shake until cold, then fine strain into a chilled highball glass. Dust some cocoa powder on top.

### ❄ Make it a White Christmas NOlada
*Replace the gold rum with pineapple juice and the coconut rum with coconut water. Swap the creme de cacao for a white chocolate syrup (not a white chocolate sauce).*

# HER MAJESTY'S FIZZ

*On the first day of Christmas my true love gave to me, some pomegranates and some bubbly*

The Royal Christmas Message is about the year's achievements, hopes for the future, and to celebrate friends and family alike. And the Pomegranate Royale is too; this combination of bubbles and pomegranate is perfect for a Christmas cheers among family, or to toast Her Majesty on another good year.

**Serves** 1 • **Method** Pour • **Glassware**

*25ml pomegranate liqueur*
*Champagne, to top*
*A few pomegranate seeds*

Add the pomegranate seeds to the champagne flute. Pour in the pomegranate liqueur and top with champagne.

### ❄ *Make it a Her Royal Temperance*
*Swap the pomegranate liqueur for pomegranate juice and top with a non-alcoholic fizz or sparkling apple juice.*

# BUTTERMILK MAPLE GIN FLIP

*On the third day of Christmas my family gave to me,
three stacks of pancakes, two drizzles of maple and a
gin flip for my brekky*

With everyone home for Christmas, a big breakfast is often on the
cards. So, you've whipped up a big stack of pancakes, drizzled
them in maple syrup, and treated everyone to a feast. But now
you've got some buttermilk leftover – what to do with it? Whip
up a Buttermilk Maple Gin Flip for a post breakfast treat and let
nothing go to waste.

**Serves** 1 • **Method** Shake • **Glassware**

*1 egg yolk
60ml gin
30ml buttermilk
15ml maple syrup*

**Garnish** *Grated fresh nutmeg*

Add the egg yolk to a cocktail shaker with two ice cubes and
shake for 10 seconds.

Open the shaker and fill it with ice. Add the gin, buttermilk and
maple syrup and shake until cold.

Strain into a coupe glass and grate some fresh nutmeg on top of
the drink.

# KENTUCKY MAPLE EGGNOG

**Eggnog is a Christmas staple, this one adds the taste of maple**

There's definitely an eggnog for everyone, and this one is for lovers of bourbon. The big bourbon notes balance well with the extra sweetness of the maple, and both fit in smoothly with the eggnog.

Serves 1 • **Method** Shake • **Glassware**

**For the cocktail**
*40ml bourbon whiskey*
*10ml (2 teaspoons) maple syrup*
*20ml quick eggnog*
*(see opposite)*

**For the quick eggnog**
*40ml whole milk (or use any milk substitute)*
*10g soft dark brown sugar*
*1 large egg, separated*
*Dash of vanilla extract*
*Pinch of salt*

**Garnish** *Grated fresh nutmeg*

To make the quick eggnog, add everything except the egg white to a bowl and beat until fully combined. Put the egg white into a separate bowl and whisk until it is foamy, then gently stir this into the other bowl. It will make about 60ml of liquid (enough for 3 cocktails).

To make the cocktail, fill a cocktail shaker with ice. Add all the ingredients and 20ml of the eggnog and shake until cold. Fine strain into a coupe glass and grate some fresh nutmeg over the top.

Using a smoother bourbon works best for balance, but a pokey bourbon will not overpower the drink, instead giving it more of a whiskey sting.

# JUNIPER FORTIFIED EGGNOG

*Come on, it's more than merry for some gin and sherry eggnog*

Flavour purists will say that eggnogs should be made with bourbon, whiskey or rum. Christmas purists would make it without the sherry and with nutmeg. But this take on the Christmas staple, more a flip than an eggnog, uses gin for a much lighter taste, and can be drunk at any time over the Christmas break. Adding the sherry not only makes it delicious but has the added advantage of lowering the overall ABV of the cocktail.

**Serves** 1  •  **Method** Shake  •  **Glassware**

*40ml London dry gin*
*20ml sherry*
*15ml pomegranate liqueur*
*15ml sugar syrup*
*1 whole egg*

Fill a cocktail shaker with ice. Add all the ingredients and shake until cold, making sure the egg has completely combined with the liquid. Fine strain into a coupe glass.

# TERRY CHRISTMAS

**Now Dasher! Now Dancer! Now Prancer, be Merry!
On Comet! On Cupid! On Donner, and Terry!**

Everyone knows a Terry. So of course, Father Christmas knows
a Terry as well; he even knows if he's been naughty or nice. The
Terry Christmas is basically a boozy, chocolate orange custard,
and tastes as delicious as you would expect it to. Just keep in
mind, once you've shaken this one up, it's not Terry's – it's yours.

**Serves** 1 • **Method** Shake • **Glassware**

*30ml gold rum*
*10ml (2 teaspoons) triple sec*
*10ml (2 teaspoons) creme de cacao white*
*1 whole egg*
*1 dash of orange bitters*

**Garnish** *Grated chocolate*

Add all the ingredients to a cocktail shaker without ice. Shake until
the egg has fully combined with the liquid. Add ice to the shaker
and shake again until cold.

Fine strain into a coupe glass and grate some chocolate on top.

# BUTTERED CUP

### Why do you shake me up (shake me up) Buttered Cup

Butter in name but not in nature, this drink is named for its
delectable buttery finish, not its flavour. The Buttered Cup is
a great use for those few near-empty bottles that are always
lingering in the back of the cupboard. It's also the perfect
accompaniment for Christmas cake, or served with any leftover
cake in the days that follow.

**Serves** 1 • **Method** Shake • **Glassware**

*45ml Scotch whisky*
*30ml oloroso sherry*
*25ml brandy*
*10ml (2 teaspoons) yellow chartreuse*
*10ml (2 teaspoons) sugar syrup*
*1 whole egg*

**To serve** *Leftover Christmas cake*

Add all the ingredients to a Cocktail Shaker without ice and shake
until the egg has completely combined with the liquid. Fill the
shaker with ice and shake again until cold.

Fine strain into a coupe glass. Get out some leftover Christmas
cake, and serve it alongside the drink.

# GREEK OLD FASHIONED

*When travels abroad are sorely missed, give a classic cocktail a Mediterranean twist*

A cocktail for those wanting a bit more than the standard traditions of the holiday period. Perfect for an afternoon or early evening, as a cold chill starts to set in. The gingerbread syrup is our connection to Christmas, but substituting Metaxa for bourbon, as featured in the classic Old Fashioned, evokes flavours of Greece and makes us dream of holidays on warmer shores.

**Serves** 1 • **Method** Stir • **Glassware**

*7.5ml (1½ teaspoons) gingerbread syrup*
*2 dashes of Angostura bitters*
*60ml Metaxa 12 liqueur*

**Garnish** *Strip of orange peel*

Add two ice cubes to an Old Fashioned glass. Add the gingerbread syrup and bitters and stir. Add the Metaxa, fill the glass to the brim with ice and stir again.

Squeeze the orange peel over the glass to release some of the oils and then add it to the drink.

# JOLLY OLD FASHIONED

*Jolly old St Nicholas, lean your ear this way, let's make Christmas cocktails the Old Fashioned way*

The classic Old Fashioned cocktail has been good this year – Santa has come to visit. And in the stocking hanging by the fireplace he's left some delicious rum and chocolate-infused bourbon – and he didn't forget the gingerbread. This Jolly Old Fashioned is perfect for Christmas night, when one muses over the gifts one has received.

Serves 1  •  Method Stir  •  Glassware

**For the cocktail**
*30ml 12–15-year aged rum*
*30ml bourbon whiskey chocolate infusion (see oposite)*
*7.5ml (1½ teaspoons) gingerbread syrup*
*3 dashes of chocolate bitters (optional)*

**For the bourbon whiskey chocolate infusion**
*120ml bourbon whiskey*
*50g cacao nibs*
*½ vanilla pod, split*

**Garnish** *Strip of orange peel, 3 cloves*

To make the bourbon whiskey chocolate infusion, add all the ingredients to a lidded jar or vessel and leave it to infuse for at least 2 days. You can leave it to infuse for up to 3 weeks – the longer it infuses, the deeper the chocolate taste will be in the bourbon. Once you are happy with the strength of the infusion, strain out the cacao nibs and vanilla. This makes about 120ml – enough for 4 cocktails. It will keep in a sterilised, sealed bottle or jar for up to a month, if not all used immediately.

To make the cocktail, fill a mixing glass with ice. Add all the ingredients and stir until cold. Strain into an Old Fashioned glass filled with ice.

Take a long strip of orange peel and stud with three cloves, pushing them through the peel. Twist over the top of the drink and drop into the glass.

# GINGERBREAD MARTINI

● ● ● ● ● ● ● ● ● ● ● ● ● ● ● ● ● ● ● ● ● ● ● ● ● ● ● ● ● ● ● ● ● ● ● ● ●

***Run, run, as fast as you can, you can't catch me, I'm the Gingerbread Martini***

During Christmas, 'afters' means different things to different people. For some it means the biggest cheeseboard known to man, for others it's devouring a whole lot of gingerbread. If the latter struck a chord, then this martini is for you; its festive dose of gingerbread and almond will help usher in the Christmas season.

**Serves** 1 • **Method** Stir • **Glassware**

*60ml vodka*
*30ml dry vermouth*
*7.5ml (1½ teaspoons) amaretto*
*7.5ml (1½ teaspoons) gingerbread syrup*

**To serve** *Ginger cookie*

Fill a mixing glass with ice. Add all the ingredients and stir.

Strain into a chilled martini glass and serve with a crisp ginger cookie alongside.

# SLEIGHBELL SLING

● ● ● ● ● ● ● ● ● ● ● ● ● ● ● ● ● ● ● ● ● ● ● ● ● ● ● ● ● ● ● ● ● ● ● ● ● ●

### *Jingle bell time is a swell time, to go slingin' in a one glass sleigh*

The Singapore Sling is quoted as being the drink where no two are alike. This Christmas version of it is definitely unique – swapping in cranberry juice and elderflower is a particular festive touch. Perfect for your Christmas party, and if you're feeling extra fancy, you can replace the soda water with any Champagne left over from your Christmas toast.

**Serves** 1 ● **Method** Stir ● **Glassware**

*50ml gin*
*50ml cranberry juice*
*3 sage leaves*

*12.5ml (2½ teaspoons)*
*elderflower cordial*
*Soda water, to top*

**Garnish** *A sprig of sage*

Crack some ice by smashing some ice cubes (you're looking for large pieces from the cubes, not snow) and then fill a highball glass with the cracked ice. Add all the ingredients and churn slowly with a bar spoon. Top with soda water and add a sprig of sage to the top of the drink.

### ❄ *Make it a NO-Weighbell Sling*
*Replace the gin with a juniper 'tea' – steep 1 tablespoon of juniper berries in 100ml boiling water for 10 minutes, strain the berries and add a teaspoon of honey to sweeten. This will make 100ml, enough for 2 drinks.*

# CHRISTMAS-SPICED WHITE RUSSIAN

*A White Russian made with Christmas spice is guaranteed to have you feeling nice*

A Christmas evening needs a nightcap, and there's no better than a White Russian, the quick and simple tipple made popular by the 1998 film *The Big Lebowski*. Your friends and family will definitely abide by this Christmas version. Bring these out as the evening draws to a close and they'll really tie the room together.

**Serves** 1 • **Method** Stir • **Glassware**

### For the cocktail
*25ml Christmas-spiced syrup (see opposite)*
*25ml vodka*
*25ml coffee liqueur*
*Milk, to top (or use any milk substitute)*

### For the Christmas-spiced syrup
*500g sugar*
*250ml water*
*1 vanilla pod, split*
*2 tablespoons ground cinnamon*
*1 tablespoon freshly grated nutmeg*

To make the Christmas-spiced syrup, add all the ingredients to a saucepan, place over a medium heat and bring to a simmer. Simmer for 10 minutes, then take it off the heat and leave until cool. This makes about 250ml syrup – enough for 10 cocktails. It will keep in the fridge in a sterilised, sealed bottle or jar for up to a week, if not all used immediately.

To make the cocktail, fill an Old Fashioned glass with ice. Add 25ml of the spiced syrup, followed by the vodka and coffee liqueur, and then top with milk.

## ❄ *Make it a Big NO-bowski*

*Replace the vodka with 20ml water and 5ml almond extract. Replace the coffee liqueur with 15ml freshly made espresso.*

# BLACK FOREST MOJITO

### If you go down in the woods today, you'll find a mojito in disguise

One of the most famous rum-based highballs gets a Christmas makeover. The Black Forest Mojito swaps out the traditional soda for cherry cola, and the sugar for blackcurrant jam. Fresh, fruity and rich in flavour – definitely a tipple to freshen up with.

**Serves** 1 • **Method** Stir • **Glassware**

50ml rum
25ml lemon juice
8 mint leaves

Spoonful of blackcurrant jam
Cherry cola, to top

**Garnish** A mini candy cane

Add the rum, lemon juice, mint leaves and blackcurrant jam to a highball glass. Add crushed ice and churn with a bar spoon. Add cherry cola to top and hang a mini candy cane over the rim of the glass.

White, dark or gold rum will all work – the flavour of the drink will change based on which rum you use.

### ❄ Make it a Black Forest NOjito
*Replace the rum with 30ml water and 5ml either rum or vanilla extract. You might also want to reduce the lemon juice to 15ml for balance.*

# NOT YOUR GRANDAD'S CUP OF TEA

*A drink of cognac, port and berry – could there be anything more merry?*

'Extravagant' goes out the window at Christmas time – 'tis the season to treat yourself. Hence the over-decorating of the house, the reappearance of all the Christmas cushions, and the opening of those special bottles for drinks. This one is a special drink, best served in your fanciest teacup, sipped slowly over time, and paired with a delectable cheeseboard. Just be careful Grandad doesn't confuse it for his tea.

**Serves** 1 • **Method** Stir • **Glassware**

*20ml cognac*
*20ml port*
*20ml raspberry liqueur*
*45ml black tea*

**Garnish** *Orange zest twist*

Fill a mixing glass with ice. Add all the ingredients and stir. Strain into a teacup filled with ice, zest with an orange twist and place the twist into the drink.

# THE COCKTAILS OF CHRISTMAS PAST

# ALASKA

● ● ● ● ● ● ● ● ● ● ● ● ● ● ● ● ● ● ● ● ● ● ● ● ● ● ● ● ● ● ● ● ● ● ● ●

***When it's getting too heated and you can't hear yourself think, stir yourself an Alaska, and sip this delightful drink***

A cocktail that should be as cold and as clear as a frozen Alaskan river, but don't confuse its clarity with weakness – this is a potent one. Just like skating on thin ice, balance is everything, so tread carefully. This drink is for sipping slowly and escaping the overheating occasions that Christmas can bring.

**Serves** 1 ● **Method** Stir ● **Glassware**

*60ml London dry gin*
*20ml yellow chartreuse*
*2 dashes of orange bitters*

**Garnish** *Lemon twist*

Fill a mixing glass with ice. Add all the ingredients and stir. Strain into a coupe glass and add the lemon twist.

This works best with a London dry gin but was originally concocted with an Old Tom in mind. So, if it ends up too dry for your tastes, swap out the London dry for an Old Tom which has a natural sweetness.

# ALEXANDER

### A festive dream of gin and double cream

The Alexander was the precursor to the slightly more well known Brandy Alexander. The notes of cacao and cream suggest this is a drink for the latter hours of a Christmas evening, but chocolate-lovers could drink this any time.

**Serves** 1 • **Method** Shake • **Glassware**

*45ml London dry gin*
*30ml creme de cacao white*
*30ml double cream*

**Garnish** *Freshly grated nutmeg, ground cinnamon*

Fill a cocktail shaker with ice, add all the ingredients and shake until cold. Strain into a chilled coupe glass and dust freshly grated nutmeg and ground cinnamon over the top.

You could also use a barrel-aged gin for more depth of flavour and an oaky taste, if it suits, and you have some to hand (yes you, gin enthusiasts!).

### ❄ Make it an Alexander the Temperate

*Swap the gin for a non-alcoholic botanical spirit – this is important to keep the balance of the drink. Replace the creme de cacao with a white chocolate syrup (not a white chocolate sauce).*

# BRANDY ALEXANDER

**Chocolate and brandy is fine and dandy**

The Brandy Alexander is rich and creamy, with subtle chocolate notes. It's a treat usually best for the later evening, but when all the holiday hours seem to blend together, no one will be judged for getting into this one a little earlier. Just don't go and spoil your Christmas dinner.

**Serves** 1 • **Method** Shake • **Glassware**

*45ml brandy*
*30ml creme de cacao white*
*30ml double cream*

**Garnish** *Freshly grated nutmeg, ground cinnamon*

Fill a cocktail shaker with ice, add all the ingredients and shake until cold.

Strain into a coupe glass and dust with freshly grated nutmeg and ground cinnamon.

# SNOWBALL

· · · · · · · · · · · · · · · · · · · · · · · · · · · · · · · · · · · · · · ·

*A simple and fresh delight, just like getting in a snowball fight*

There was a period where it felt like everyone had a bottle of the Dutch drink advocaat. And the combination of advocaat and lemonade, the Snowball, is perched atop many 'drinks you'll remember if you grew up in the 80s' lists, and for good reason. Both sparkling bright and warmly creamy, it's the perfect drink for the idyllic dusk hours of Christmastime, before the colder and darker winter months set in.

Serves 1 • Method Stir • Glassware

*50ml advocaat*
*50ml sparkling lemonade*

**Garnish** *Maraschino cherry or lemon slice*

Fill a highball glass with ice. Add the advocaat and sparkling lemonade and stir gently until the glass becomes cold. Garnish with a maraschino cherry or lemon slice – or both.

# SIR CHARLES PUNCH

*A good recipe can age just like a fine wine – this classic dates back to 1949*

As classic as cocktails can get – the original recipe comes from a late 1940s edition of the *Esquire's Handbook for Hosts*, which suggests it should be served at Christmas. This tipple is short, but full of personality.

**Serves** 1 • **Method** Stir • **Glassware**

*30ml tawny port (10-year-old)*
*15ml cognac VSOP*
*15ml orange liqueur (I used Grand Marnier)*
*5ml (1 teaspoon) sugar syrup*

**Garnish** *Orange zest twist*

Fill a mixing glass with ice, add all the ingredients and stir. Strain into an Old Fashioned glass filled with ice.

Zest the glass with the orange twist, and then add it to the drink.

# HARRISON'S EGGNOG

*To keep the fire going, go add another log; keep the party going with this delicious eggnog*

Named after William Henry Harrison, who was US president in 1841 for only a month before passing away, giving him the title of serving the shortest presidency in US history. His favourite drink was said to be eggnog, and this apple and brandy version is a twist on his old recipe.

**Serves** 1  •  **Method** Shake  •  **Glassware**

*60ml apple brandy*
*15ml sugar syrup*
*1 whole egg*
*50ml apple cider*

**Garnish** *Grated fresh nutmeg*

Fill a cocktail shaker with ice. Add all the ingredients except the cider and shake until cold, making sure the egg has completely combined with the liquid.

Add the cider to an Old Fashioned glass without ice, and then strain the contents of the cocktail shaker into the glass. Grate fresh nutmeg across the top.

# TOM AND JERRY

**This hot Tom and Jerry is an old-time drink used by one and all to celebrate Christmas**

Despite its name, this tipple isn't inspired by the classic cat and mouse duo. Instead, it was created to publicise a play in the 1820s, named after its main characters Jerry Hawthorn and Corinthian Tom. It's such a crowd-pleaser that an old joke suggests Christmas was only invented as an excuse to drink them.

Serves 1 • **Method** Mix, in a large bowl • **Glassware**

### For the cocktail
*30ml Jamaican rum (I used Appleton 12)*
*45ml cognac VSOP*
*30ml egg and spice mixture (see opposite)*

### For the egg and spice mixture
*2 eggs, separated*
*80g caster sugar*
*2 pinches of ground cinnamon*
*2 pinches of ground cloves*
*3 pinches of grated nutmeg*

**Garnish** *Grated fresh nutmeg*

Prewarm a toddy glass with hot water and set aside.

To make the egg and spice mixture, whisk the egg yolks in a bowl, then add the sugar and spices and whisk thoroughly again. In a separate bowl, whisk the egg whites to a froth, then add to the main mixture. This makes about 180ml of spice mixture –

enough for 6 cocktails. It will keep in the fridge in a sterilised, sealed bottle or jar for 1–2 days, if not all used immediately.

To make the cocktail, add the rum and cognac to the warmed toddy glass. Add 30ml of the egg and spice mixture and top with boiling water. As the head of the drink becomes frothy, grate some fresh nutmeg on top.

# THE MORE
# THE MERRIER

# MULLED WINE

● ● ● ● ● ● ● ● ● ● ● ● ● ● ● ● ● ● ● ● ● ● ● ● ● ● ● ● ● ● ● ● ● ● ● ● ● ● ● ●

***Mulled wine, feeling fine, drink with friends and pass the time***

Mulled wine is a Christmas classic. But, like Christmas, this one has a lot of moving parts, so make it for when everyone sits down for a bit of respite. With all the family, presents, bad sweaters and terrible puns, this recipe will help you mull things over.

**Serves** 6 ● **Method** Mix, in a large saucepan ● **Glassware**

*750ml (1 bottle) red wine*
*1 clementine, sliced*
*1 cinnamon stick*
*1 star anise*
*3 dried figs*
*4 cloves*
*3 black peppercorns*
*50ml brandy (optional)*

Pour the red wine into a large saucepan. Add all the ingredients (except for the brandy) and place over a low heat. Heat until simmering and then turn off the heat. Strain the mixture through a sieve to get rid of the whole spices. Slowly stir in the brandy, if using, and then ladle the mulled wine into coffee mugs.

Adding the brandy is optional – don't include it to make this a less boozy mulled wine. Just remember to stir the mixture, with or without the brandy, before serving.

# CHRISTMAS COSMOPOLITAN PUNCH

*There ain't no party like a cosmo party before a lunch that's hearty and more*

A punch for a festive lunch, this is a Christmas take on the *Sex and the City* favourite, the Cosmo. Perfect for sitting around with friends and discussing who is more of a Samantha and who is definitely not a Carrie.

**Serves** 10 • **Method** Mix, in a jug • **Glassware**

*500ml vodka*
*500ml ginger wine*
*1 litre cranberry juice*
*30ml lime juice*
*5 slices of fresh ginger*

**Garnish** *Lime zest peel*

Add the vodka and ginger wine to a jug filled with ice and stir. Add the cranberry juice, lime juice and ginger slices, stirring each in separately. Strain into martini glasses and zest each glass with the lime zest, discarding the peel after use.

### ❄ Make it a Christmas CosNOpolitan Punch
*Swap the vodka for a non-alcoholic white spirit and the ginger wine for a non-alcoholic ginger beer, giving this punch a fizzy, spicy edge.*

# EGGNOG

$\bullet\bullet\bullet\bullet\bullet\bullet\bullet\bullet\bullet\bullet\bullet\bullet\bullet\bullet\bullet\bullet\bullet\bullet\bullet\bullet\bullet\bullet\bullet\bullet\bullet\bullet\bullet\bullet\bullet\bullet\bullet\bullet\bullet\bullet\bullet\bullet\bullet$

***Deck the house with eggnogs 'plenty, fa-la-la-la-la, la-la-la-la***

***This recipe makes more than twenty, fa-la-la-la-la, la-la-la-la***

A cocktail that started life in Europe, eggnog was traditionally drunk by only the upper classes, as eggs were scarce. Its association with Christmas came about when the drink made its way to America in the 1700s. This big, delicious recipe is for when everyone has retired from the dinner table and is ready to get stuck into a Christmas game before falling asleep on the sofas.

**Serves** 24 • **Method** Mix, in a large bowl • **Glassware**

*12 large eggs, separated*
*200g soft dark brown sugar*
*Dash of vanilla extract*
*Pinch of salt*
*1 litre milk (or use any milk substitute)*
*250ml gold rum*
*250ml brandy*

**Garnish** *Freshly grated nutmeg*

Put the egg yolks, sugar, vanilla, salt and milk into a large bowl and beat until it is the consistency of cream. Add the rum and brandy.

In a separate bowl, beat the egg whites into a froth, and then add them to the large mixing bowl. Stir and pour into coffee mugs, then grate fresh nutmeg over the top of each one.

Using milk substitutes, like oat or almond, will change the overall flavour of the eggnog, but will still make a delicious drink.

## ❄ Make it EggNOg

*Leave out the rum and the brandy and cut the sugar in half. Bear in mind with the absence of the alcohol it becomes sickly sweet, so is best served in a teacup and sipped slowly.*

# WHITE CARGO

· · · · · · · · · · · · · · · · · · · · · · · · · · · · · · · · · · · · ·

***Jingle bell dreams, filled with ice cream, to drink the night away***

Booze and ice cream – what's not to love? Ice-cream cocktails are always popular and very straightforward. Serve these alongside the pudding course of a Christmas dinner, and you'll be the life of the party.

**Serves** 20 • **Method** Mix, in a large bowl • **Glassware**

*700ml gin*
*2 litres vanilla ice cream*
*180ml maraschino liqueur*

**Garnish** *Freshly grated nutmeg*

Add all the ingredients to a large bowl. Wait until the ice cream has mostly melted and then stir. Serve in coffee mugs and grate fresh nutmeg over the top of each drink.

# WHITE CHRISTMAS MARGARITA

### I'm dreaming of a White Christmas, with margaritas nice and cold

White Christmases are few and far between, but there's no denying a bit of snow is a magical addition to an already festive time. So why not do the same with some margaritas and add a little white Christmas magic? Creamy and slightly sweet, without removing the bite and tang of a margarita, these White Christmas Margaritas will have everyone happily snowed under.

**Serves** 6 • **Method** Blend • **Glassware**

*340ml tequila*
*225ml triple sec*
*400ml coconut milk*
*125ml lime juice*

**Garnish** *Lime slices, handful of fresh cranberries*

Add all the ingredients to a blender with two scoops of crushed ice and blend until combined. Pour the blended mix into Old Fashioned glasses and add a couple of cranberries and a lime slice to each one.

# WHISKY CREAM

● ● ● ● ● ● ● ● ● ● ● ● ● ● ● ● ● ● ● ● ● ● ● ● ● ● ● ● ● ● ● ● ●

### *I don't care about the presents, just make me a Whisky Cream*

This recipe for whisky cream, from whisky expert Andrea Montague, is an absolute gift. Creamy, boozy, deliciously rich and absolutely moreish, this is the drink you'll get for Christmas and spend the whole next year thinking about. Perfect for bottling up and keeping chilled, it will make delicious gifts for friends and family to take home – just make sure you save enough for yourself.

**Serves** 3–4  ●  **Method** Stir, in a bain-marie  ●  **Glassware**

*150g dark chocolate (at least 70% cocoa solids)*
*250ml condensed milk*
*60ml freshly made espresso*
*80ml double cream*
*350ml whisky (I used Aberfeldy 12-year-old)*
*45ml vanilla extract*
*15ml almond extract*

Melt the dark chocolate in a bain-marie over a low-medium heat. Add the condensed milk and stir thoroughly, then add the espresso and cream and stir thoroughly again. Slowly add the whisky, little by little, stirring as it is added. Add the extracts, stir again, and take off the heat to cool.

Once it is cold, ladle into Old Fashioned glasses filled with ice. You can bottle and chill it as well, and it will last for about a month in a sealed, sterilised bottle. If you're bottling it, give it a good shake before serving.

### ❄️ Make it a Christmas Cream

*You can replace the whisky with a non-alcoholic aromatic or non-alcoholic grain spirit. Otherwise, this is still tasty if you leave out the whisky entirely; bear in mind it should then be drunk the same day as being made, as the alcohol acts as a preservative.*

# BREWSKI ROYALESKI

**Spruce up a couple of beers and give your friends some Christmas cheers**

You're feeling like a beer but craving something a bit fancier. Well, this is the season for it. The Brewski Royaleski is the drink for après ski, or just when you're making the transition from beer to cocktail. When it comes to what beer to use – wheat beers, dark lagers, white stouts, Belgian sours and lighter lagers work best. But use what you've got, really. Just make sure both beers are the same type.

**Serves** 2–3 • **Method** Stir, in a glass jug • **Glassware**

*125ml raspberry liqueur (I used Chambord)*
*25ml lemon juice*
*25ml lime cordial*
*2 bottles of beer (should be the same beer)*

**Garnish** *A few handfuls of fresh cranberries*

Fill a glass jug with ice. Add the raspberry liqueur, lemon juice and lime cordial, and then pour in the two beers. Stir thoroughly and pour into highball glasses. Garnish each glass with a handful of cranberries.

### ❄️ *Make it a Flagon on the Wagon*
*Swap the raspberry liqueur for a raspberry syrup and top with your preferred choice of non-alcoholic beer.*

# SANTA AU CHAMPAGNE

*He's gonna whip up something naughty and nice*

A slightly naughty and deliciously nice twist on the Soyer Au Champagne, this is a late-night dessert cocktail for you and the family to tuck into. Blending with the champagne aerates the ice cream and makes it soft and fluffy. You could use another type of bubbly to achieve a similar effect, but you'd then have to call this drink Sparkling Santa Wine.

**Serves** 4  •  **Method** Blend  •  **Glassware**

*240ml cider brandy (Calvados or cognac will also work)*
*4 scoops of vanilla ice cream*
*60ml curaçao (or use triple sec)*
*60ml sugar syrup*
*300ml champagne*

**Garnish** *Angostura bitters*

Add all ingredients to a blender and blend on high speed for 10–20 seconds. Pour into coupe glasses and add a dash of Angostura bitters to each drink.

# FISH HOUSE PUNCH

*Some celebrate with a spread for lunch, others just whip up a Fish House Punch*

One of this drink's supposed origins is that it was made in the 1840s to celebrate women being allowed into the Fish House in Philadelphia, for the first time for a Christmas party. Hence, Fish House Punch is traditionally made in larger quantities and served in a punchbowl.

**Serves** 6 • **Method** Mix, in a punchbowl • **Glassware**

*180ml gold rum*
*180ml cognac VSOP*
*135ml peach liqueur*
*270ml cold black English breakfast tea*
*120ml lemon juice*
*45ml sugar syrup*

**Garnish** *Lemon slices, freshly grated nutmeg*

Add all the ingredients to a punchbowl. Add ice and stir to combine.

Ladle into Old Fashioned glasses filled with ice and add a lemon slice and some grated nutmeg on top of each one.

# DRINKING IN A WINTER WONDERLAND

# BLACK VELVET

* * * * * * * * * * * * * * * * * * * * * * * * * * * * * * * * * * * * *

*Some pairings cause troubles, but not Guinness and bubbles*

A drink for late December, the Black Velvet was created to mourn the death of Prince Albert, husband of Queen Victoria. The combination of flavours is unique, and perfect for a cold winter's evening, when you're craving something bubblier than a stout, but more warming than a glass of fizz.

**Serves** 1 • **Method** Stir • **Glassware**

*105ml stout (I used Guinness)*
*Brut champagne, to top*

**Garnish** *A shamrock or mint leaf*

Slowly pour the stout into a chilled champagne glass, and then slowly top with the champagne. Gently stir. Garnish with a shamrock or mint leaf on the rim of the glass.

You can replace the Guinness with any other stout, for a different flavour combination.

# HOT GIN COLLINS

• • • • • • • • • • • • • • • • • • • • • • • • • • • • • • • • • • • •

**A simple one to add to the list, keep yourself warm with gin collins twist**

When it comes to warming ourselves up, sometimes simple is best. Straightforward, warm and juniper-forward, this one is perfect for the late nights when sweaters and beanies just aren't cutting it.

**Serves** 1 • **Method** Stir • **Glassware**

*40ml London dry gin*
*25ml lemon juice*
*25ml sugar syrup*
*Hot water, to top*

**Garnish** *Lemon wheel, cinnamon stick*

Add all the ingredients to a coffee mug and top with hot (not boiling) water. Stir, then garnish with a lemon wheel and a whole cinnamon stick.

# HOT TODDY

**When the winter blues start to get you down, this drink will turn your frown upside down**

A Hot Toddy is the perfect drink for when you're feeling a bit blue or have come down with a cold or the flu. The warm notes of the whisky combine well with the cloves and honey, and a little sugar syrup takes the edge of the lemon. Using a honey-styled whisky complements the honey well, but any whisky will suffice.

**Serves** 1  •  **Method** Stir  •  **Glassware**

*45ml Scotch whisky*
*10ml (2 teaspoons) lemon juice*
*10ml (2 teaspoons) honey*
*5ml (1 teaspoon) sugar syrup*
*3 dried cloves*
*Boiling water, to top*

**Garnish** *Cinnamon stick*

Prewarm a toddy glass and set aside while you bring a kettle of water to boil.

Add all the ingredients to the toddy glass and add the boiling water. Stir thoroughly and add a cinnamon stick.

If you don't have a toddy glass, just use a coffee or tea mug.

❄ *Make it a Hot NOddy*

*Replace the whisky with 5ml (1 teaspoon) vanilla extract.*

　　　　　　　　　　**Drinking in a Winter Wonderland** ●

# HOT BUTTERED RUM

**I shall make for you, Hot and Buttered Rum, pa-rum pum pum rum!**

The Hot Buttered Rum is like a warm grilled cheese sandwich. Except without the bread, the cheese or using the grill at all. Yet, somehow, it accomplishes that same feeling – comfort, warmth and deliciousness. For an extra boozy touch, replace the boiling water with hot cider.

**Serves** 1  •  **Method** Mix  •  **Glassware**

*10ml (2 teaspoons) honey*
*60ml gold rum*
*Small slice of unsalted butter*
*Freshly grated nutmeg*
*Hot water, to top*

**Garnish** *Cinnamon stick, slice of lemon*

Warm a toddy glass and add the honey. Add the rum, butter and nutmeg and top with hot (not boiling) water. Stir until the honey and butter are dissolved. Add the cinnamon stick and lemon slice garnishes.

You could also serve in a coffee mug instead of a toddy glass, if it suits.

# GIN AND (HOT) JUICE

**When it's cold outside and you want to stay in, warm up the cider and open the gin**

A rapper once described the combination of gin and juice as a tipple to sip on when you're laid back and your mind is on other things. Sounds perfect for a wintery evening, especially when the cider has been warmed up. Gin and (Hot) Juice fans would know that traditionally Seagrams would be the gin of choice, with Tanqueray a close second.

**Serves** 1 • **Method** Mix, in a saucepan • **Glassware**

*100ml hard apple cider*
*30ml gin*
*20ml apple brandy or Calvados*
*10ml (2 teaspoons) lemon juice*
*5ml (1 teaspoon) honey*

Add the cider to a pan and warm over a medium heat.

Take off the heat and add the other ingredients. Stir until the honey has combined with the liquid and pour into a coffee mug.

# AMARETTO SOUR

●●●●●●●●●●●●●●●●●●●●●●●●●●●●●●●●●●●●●●

**Cometh the winter, cometh dark hour, cometh the buzz of an Amaretto Sour**

There's a particular buzz to being comfortably warm during the winter months. Whether it's wearing that warm, comfy hoodie or sweater, sporting a snug pair of slippers or even lying on the couch under that particularly woolly blanket, there's nothing quite like it. Except, maybe, an Amaretto Sour. The frothy almond buzz and the balance between sweet and sour is as comforting as that warm blanket ever was.

**Serves** 1 • **Method** Shake • **Glassware**

60ml amaretto
30ml lemon juice
15ml egg white
1 dash of Angostura bitters

**Garnish** *Maraschino cherry on a cocktail stick*

Add all the ingredients to a cocktail shaker, without ice, and shake, making sure the egg white has completely combined with the liquid.

Fill the shaker with ice and shake again until cold. Strain into an Old Fashioned glass filled with ice and garnish with a maraschino cherry resting across the glass on a cocktail stick.

### ❄ Make it a AmarettNO Sour

*Swap the amaretto for a non-alcoholic amaretto or orgeat syrup. Alternatively make an almond syrup by adding 5ml almond extract to 115ml sugar syrup – this makes enough for 2 drinks.*

# KING OF ROSES

**For drinks in winter just follow your noses to the aromas of citrus and the allure of the roses**

Created one holiday period in a tiny, London cocktail bar called Casita that had surpluses of bourbon and citrus. The King of Roses is the exemplary cocktail for how festive flavour can really enhance a drink. The citrus and the deep, oak notes of the bourbon pair excellently, and despite it being a cold drink, the warming notes from the gingerbread syrup make this cocktail one that warms from inside out. You could use another bourbon, but you couldn't still call it the King of Roses.

Serves 1 • Method Shake • Glassware

*50ml Four Roses bourbon whiskey*
*25ml ginger liqueur*
*50ml orange juice*
*25ml lemon juice*
*10ml (2 teaspoons) gingerbread syrup*

Fill a cocktail shaker with ice. Add all the ingredients and shake until cold. Fine strain into a coupe glass.

# WINTER SANGRIA

### This main from Spain, tweaked for days full of rain

Sangria is a party drink, and this winter twist is no exception. The word *sangria* in Spanish translates as 'bloodletting' – apt for a drink best shared with friends while letting off some steam.

**Serves** 6  •  **Method** Stir, in a large jug  •  **Glassware**

750ml (1 bottle) dry red wine
60ml triple sec
60ml brandy
1 orange, sliced
1 lemon, sliced
1 pear, sliced
Seeds from ½ pomegranate
2 cinnamon sticks
175ml ginger ale

Add all the ingredients, except the ginger ale, to a large jug and stir to combine. Cover, and place in fridge for 1–2 hours.

When you are ready to serve, add the ginger ale to the mixture. Stir, and pour into wine glasses, making sure some of the sliced fruit is in each glass.

# DARK AND CAFFEINATED

● ● ● ● ● ● ● ● ● ● ● ● ● ● ● ● ● ● ● ● ● ● ● ● ● ● ● ● ● ● ● ● ● ● ●

*Through the winter the sun sets quicker, so keep the day going with some caffeine and liquor*

We've all been there – the sun is setting, it's getting dark, we check the time – but it's still only the afternoon. The struggle is real. So, it comes to decision time – coffee, or something stronger – unless we could just combine the two? This caffeinated take on the Dark and Stormy is perfect for those long, winter afternoons.

**Serves** 1 ● **Method** Stir ● **Glassware**

*40ml dark rum (I used Gosling's)*
*15ml tequila reposado*
*Ginger beer, to top*
*30ml freshly made espresso*

Fill a highball glass with ice. Add the rum and tequila. Stir and top with the ginger beer, then slowly pour in the espresso.

# AN ERNEST WINTER

**A drink that teases a warmer season, but do you really need a reason?**

Daiquiris are traditionally for the warmer seasons, but why should spring and summer have all the fun? An Ernest Winter is a Hemmingway special, adapted for those weekends in winter where we embrace the crisp freshness of cold air, while having one eye on the arrival of warmer days.

**Serves** 1  •  **Method** Shake  •  **Glassware**

*50ml white rum*
*15ml pomegranate liqueur*
*20ml lime juice*
*15ml pink grapefruit juice*
*Ginger beer, to top*

**Garnish** *½ slice of pink grapefruit, a few pomegranate seeds*

Fill a cocktail shaker with ice. Add all the ingredients except the ginger beer and shake until cold. Strain into an Old Fashioned glass filled with ice, and top with ginger beer.

Garnish with half a slice of pink grapefruit, topped with a couple of pomegranate seeds.

### ❄️ *Make it an Ernest Spring*
*Leave out the rum and replace the pomegranate liqueur with a pomegranate syrup.*

# GIGI AND T

**Gin and tonics will never go wrong, but drink this when the winter feels too long**

If there was ever a season to embrace sloe berries, it's winter. Sloe gin is, however, a little too heavy on its own with tonic, so the addition of the dry gin lightens things up. Simple and well balanced, this little tipple goes down extremely easily after a long day at work.

**Serves** 1 • **Method** Stir • **Glassware**

*30ml London dry gin*
*20ml sloe gin*
*Tonic water, to top*

**Garnish** *Slice of lemon, a few juniper berries*

Fill a Copa de Balon glass with ice. Add the dry and sloe gins and top with tonic. Stir, and garnish with a lemon slice and a few juniper berries.

# WINTER WHISKEY SOUR

*Well in the kitchen we can go and build a sour*

A drink that became big during Prohibition in the United States, the Whiskey Sour is now a cocktail staple the world over. This version has been tinkered with specifically for drinking during winter – the addition of orange juice and honey help brighten and freshen up the drink. Perfect for keeping us going strong until brighter, fresher days roll in.

**Serves** 1 • **Method** Shake • **Glassware**

*50ml bourbon whiskey*
*7.5ml (1½ teaspoons) lemon juice*
*7.5ml (1½ teaspoons) orange juice*
*5ml (1 teaspoon) sugar syrup*
*5ml (1 teaspoon) honey*
*1 egg white*

**Garnish** *Honey, gold edible glitter (optional),* slice of orange

Rim an Old Fashioned glass with honey and dip in gold edible glitter.

Fill a cocktail shaker with ice and add all the ingredients. Shake until cold, ensuring the egg white has completely combined with the rest of the liquid. Fill the prepared glass with ice, strain the cocktail, and add an orange slice.

The addition of the edible gold glitter for the rim is entirely optional, but makes it a brighter, fancier-looking tipple.

## ❄ *Make it a Winter Sour*

*Swap the bourbon whiskey for 45ml water and 5ml vanilla extract.*

# WINTER SIDECAR

● ● ● ● ● ● ● ● ● ● ● ● ● ● ● ● ● ● ● ● ● ● ● ● ● ● ● ● ● ● ● ● ● ● ● ● ● ●

**To survive the season of snow and ice, try this classic with some seasonal spice**

The Sidecar cocktail dates back to around the end of World War 1, and it is commonly debated which city should claim invention of the drink – Paris, or London. What isn't debated is that it is a boozy drink, balanced on the side of tart. Some bartenders will say serving it a sugar-rimmed glass is essential – this version opts for a winter twist of a cinnamon rim and the inclusion of clementine juice instead.

**Serves** 1 ● **Method** Shake ● **Glassware**

*50ml cognac*
*30ml dry vermouth*
*15ml clementine juice*

**Garnish** *Clementine juice and ground cinnamon*

Rim a coupe glass with clementine juice and dip in ground cinnamon. Set the glass aside.

Fill a cocktail shaker with ice. Add all the ingredients and shake until cold, then fine strain into the prepared glass.

If you can't find clementine juice, you could just use orange juice instead, and add 1–2 teaspoons of sugar syrup.

# SLOE FALLING ON SODAS

*A pretty and tranquil drink to make, but go sloe and steady with the shake*

This wintery take on the Ramos Fizz uses sloe gin to add seasonal flavour and colour. The catch with this drink, as with a Ramos, is that it requires a very long shake, but you'll be rewarded with a delicious, souffle-like texture. This is the cocktail to shake some spectacle and freshness into your winter.

Serves 1  •  Method Shake  •  Glassware

*60ml sloe gin*
*20ml whole milk (or use any milk substitute)*
*15ml lemon juice*
*10ml (2 teaspoons) lime juice*
*10ml (2 teaspoons) sugar syrup*
*1 egg white*
*30ml soda water*

Fill a cocktail shaker with ice. Add all the ingredients, except for the soda water, and shake for 7 minutes (wrap a tea towel around the shaker to stop it getting too cold to hold). It's not necessary to shake non-stop for 7 minutes, just for 7 minutes total. Once shaken, leave the shaker to rest for around 2 minutes.

Strain the cocktail into the highball glass at the same time as pouring the soda; this will create a fizzy and foamy effect. Fill the glass until about three-quarters full. Put the glass in the fridge for

1 minute, letting the foam settle and get cold. Remove the glass and make a hole in the middle of the foam with a straw. Pour the remaining cocktail into the hole so that the foam rises up the glass. You are aiming to get a couple of centimetres of foam head above the glass. (A straight-sided highball glass will work best.)

A couple of extra notes on this method – open the shaker first over the sink, after shaking, to make sure the cocktail doesn't pour out everywhere due to the dilution from being shaken with ice for so long. Try and team up with another person, if possible, for the long shake, to lighten the load.

### ❄ Make it a SNOw Falling on Sodas

*Swap the sloe gin for a blackberry jam syrup: add 5 tablespoons blackberry jam and 2 tablespoons water to a small saucepan and put over a medium heat. Use a whisk to stir thoroughly until you have a syrup-like texture (makes enough for 2–3 drinks).*

# FRIGHTFUL DELIGHTS FOR HALLOWEEN NIGHT

# CANDIED APPLE MOPED

### A candied apple a day keeps the monsters away

Candied apples have long been sweets of the trick or treat variety, as apple harvests traditionally fall in the Halloween season. This sweet, Halloween riff on a vesper martini is the perfect treat for Halloween guests. It might not be as fancy as its inspiration, but it'll still get you where you need to go.

**Serves** 1 • **Method** Stir • **Glassware**

*60ml London dry gin*
*20ml salted caramel vodka*
*20ml apple brandy (I used Avallen Calvados)*

**Garnish** *A very thin slice of apple*

Fill a mixing glass with ice. Add all the ingredients and stir until chilled. Strain into a martini glass. Cut into a thin slice of apple so you can position it on the rim of the glass.

# PUMPKIN-SPICED RUSSIAN

*As All Hallows Eve turns to All Hallows Night, drink this Pumpkin-spiced tipple, from Russia, with fright*

Halloween and pumpkin spice go hand in hand; for every carved pumpkin by a front door there's a coffee shop serving pumpkin-spiced lattes down the street. This Pumpkin-spiced Russian is a sweet and spiced milky indulgence to treat yourself with, but fans of pumpkin spice will already know that craving well.

**Serves** 1 • **Method** Stir • **Glassware**

*60ml vodka*
*30ml coffee liqueur*
*25ml whole milk (or use any milk substitute)*

*10ml (2 teaspoons) pumpkin spice syrup*
*10ml (2 teaspoons) caramel sauce*

**Garnish** *Caramel sauce, pumpkin spice, 1 cinnamon stick*

Rim an Old Fashioned glass with caramel sauce and dip in some pumpkin spice.

Fill the glass with ice. Add all the ingredients, and churn with a small spoon, ensuring the caramel sauce is thoroughly mixed into the drink. Add a cinnamon stick to finish.

For even more pumpkin spice flavour, sprinkle some pumpkin spice across the top of the drink.

### ❄ Make it a Pumpkin-spiced Switzerland
*Replace the vodka with a non-alcoholic white spirit. Add 10ml sugar syrup and 30ml freshly made espresso in place of the coffee liqueur.*

# BLACK MAGIC

### Double, double, toil and troubles, every season needs some bubbles

*A Halloween party needs a drink for everyone to cheers with, and this glass of bubbles is magic. Despite the name, the cocktail is more peach than black in colour, and isn't as sweet as it looks.*

Serves 1 • Method Shake • Glassware

12 fresh red grapes
15ml triple sec
Brut champagne, to top

Garnish *2 black grapes*

Muddle the grapes in the bottom of a cocktail shaker. Fill the shaker with ice. Add the triple sec and shake until cold. Fine strain into a chilled champagne flute and top with the champagne.

Cut into the 2 grapes so that you can push them on to the rim of the glass.

If you're making more than one of these at a time, you can reuse the grapes in the shaker.

# BLOOD AND SAND

• • • • • • • • • • • • • • • • • • • • • • • • • • • • • • • • • • • • • •

### When you're all out of tricks and treats are in hand, shake yourself up a Blood and Sand

This appropriately blood-coloured classic from *The Savoy Cocktail Book* is a perfect drink for post Halloween celebrations. The cherry liqueur represents the 'blood', and the blood orange juice is the 'sand'.

Serves 1 • **Method** Shake • **Glassware**

*30ml whisky*
*25ml cherry liqueur*
*20ml sweet vermouth*
*20ml blood orange juice*

**Garnish** *Orange zest twist, maraschino cherry*

Fill a cocktail shaker with ice. Add all the ingredients and shake until cold. Fine strain into a chilled coupe glass.

Zest the glass with an orange twist, and then discard the twist. Finish with a maraschino cherry positioned on the rim of the glass.

Traditionally the Blood and Sand uses orange juice, so you can use that if you can't find blood oranges to juice.

# ZOMBIE

● ● ● ● ● ● ● ● ● ● ● ● ● ● ● ● ● ● ● ● ● ● ● ● ● ● ● ● ● ● ● ● ● ● ●

### *In your ha-aa-and, zombie, zombie, Zombie-ie-ie-ie*

*If there's ever an excuse to shake up a Zombie, it's Halloween.
Big, bold, and boozy, the cinnamon and passionfruit syrups tame
the combination of overproof and flavoured rums. Too many of
these and you'll definitely be groaning like a zombie.*

**Serves** 1 • **Method** Shake • **Glassware**

30ml Jamaican rum
25ml overproof rum
30ml golden rum
15ml falernum
10ml (2 teaspoons) cinnamon
syrup

5ml (1 teaspoon) passionfruit
syrup (optional)
20ml grapefruit juice
20ml lime juice
2 dashes of Angostura bitters
2 dashes of absinthe
5ml (1 teaspoon) grenadine

**Garnish** *Sprig of mint*

Fill a cocktail shaker with ice. Add all the ingredients, except for
the grenadine. Shake until cold, then strain into a hurricane glass
filled with ice. Slowly pour in the grenadine.

The mix of different rums in this drink ensures a balanced and potent
zombie with depth, but if you don't have them all, you can make a
delicious zombie with 80ml of whatever rum you have to hand.

### ❄ *Make it an Enlivener*
*Swap out the whole recipe for a cup of strong coffee.*

# HAUNTED COFFEE OF COONEEN

*Once upon a time, there was cottage haunted, and then approached a cocktail, delicious and undaunted*

This tipple is named after one of Ireland's most famous haunted houses. Part Irish coffee and part espresso martini, the Haunted Coffee of Cooneen is like a great scary story – devilishly well balanced with a twist in the tale; it's dark, caffeinated, and smooth, with a surprise finish of rum. And just like any good ghost story, having too many of these before bed will keep you up all night.

**Serves** 1 • **Method** Shake • **Glassware**

*25ml Irish whiskey*
*25ml coffee liqueur (I used Kahlua)*
*15ml dark or spiced rum*
*30ml fresh espresso*
*5ml (1 teaspoon) sugar syrup*

Fill a cocktail shaker with ice. Add all the ingredients and shake until cold. Fine strain into a coupe glass.

# SCREAMING BANANA BANSHEE

**Now is the night, for a banana banshee flavoured with a scream, just add the cream**

A banshee, according to folklore, was a spectre and an omen of bad tidings. This Screaming Banana Banshee is a banshee in name only; a combination of banana, chocolate and cream can only lead to good things.

Serves 1 • Method Blend • Glassware

45ml vodka
30ml banana liqueur
30ml creme de cacao white
45ml single cream
45ml whole milk (or use any milk substitute)
½ banana, peeled

**Garnish** A thin slice of banana

Add all the ingredients to a blender with some crushed ice and blend until combined. Pour into a tall hurricane or highball glass and position a thin slice of banana on the rim of the glass.

Using oat, coconut or almond milk will change the flavour of the drink, but it will remain a tasty combination.

❄ *Make it a Banana Banshee*
*For a less alcoholic version, you can leave out the vodka.*

# CORPSE REVIVER NO. 2

*I was working in the bar, late one night, when my eyes beheld a delicious sight*
*On Halloween a classic drink does thrive, a tasty number and a corpse reviver*

An absolute classic from *The Savoy Cocktail Book*, and one that always impresses partygoers and adult trick-or-treaters alike. It's a lot simpler to make than any mad science, and goes down very well, but take care; in its original recipe author Harry Craddock comments 'four of these taken in swift succession will unrevive the corpse again'.

**Serves** 1 • **Method** Shake • **Glassware**

*25ml London dry gin*
*25ml triple sec*
*25ml Lillet Blanc*
*25ml lemon juice*
*3 dashes of absinthe*

**Garnish** *A lemon zest peel*

Fill a cocktail shaker with ice. Add all the ingredients and shake until cold. Fine strain into a chilled coupe glass.

Zest the glass with the lemon peel and add the peel to the drink.

# DAY OF THE DEAD DELICACIES

# VAMPIRO

* * * * * * * * * * * * * * * * * * * * * * * * * * * * * * * * * * * * * *

***Out from his coffin, Dracula did go, to quench his thirst with a Vampiro***

The national drink of Mexico, where it was named the Vampiro, or 'vampire', because the drink's red colour is reminiscent of blood. A perfect appetiser for a Day of the Dead celebration, or just for a sunny late-October afternoon.

For a more traditional take, you could swap the tomato juice for pomegranate juice and make without the grenadine.

Serves 1 • **Method** Shake • **Glassware**

60ml tequila reposado
30ml tomato juice
30ml orange juice
15ml lime juice

15ml grenadine syrup
7 drops of hot pepper sauce
Pinch of salt
Grind of black pepper

**Garnish** *Lime wedge*

Fill a cocktail shaker with ice. Add all the ingredients and shake until cold. Strain into an Old Fashioned glass filled with ice and add the lime wedge.

### ❄ *Make it a Vampir-NO*
*Replace the tequila with a non-alcoholic tequila-styled spirit, or you could use a handful of fresh coriander instead.*

# ANTIGUA USANZA

### Mark the day with a Mexican-inspired Old Fashioned

Deliciously smoky and subtly sweet, with just the right amount of bite, the Antigua Usanza is twist on an Old Fashioned, inspired by the flavours of Mexico. It's a cocktail that honours the old-fashioned ways in a wonderfully localised style – perfect for Day of the Dead celebrations.

**Serves** 1 • **Method** Stir • **Glassware**

*50ml tequila reposado*
*10ml (2 teaspoons) mezcal*

*10ml (2 teaspoons) agave syrup*
*2 dashes of orange bitters*

**Garnish** *Twist of orange peel*

Fill a mixing glass with ice. Add all the ingredients and stir until chilled. Strain into an Old Fashioned glass filled with ice, zest the glass with the orange twist, then add the twist to the drink.

If you want a bit more bite, you could also add a touch of spice by adding a dash or two of habañero sauce before stirring.

And for some theatre, add a flamed orange zest over the top of your drink. To do so, take a large disc of orange peel. Face the outer side of the peel towards the drink and use matches or a lighter to warm the outside briefly. Snap the peel to release the oils through the flame and over the cocktail, resulting in a crackle of orange oils over the surface of the drink.

# BONFIRE BREWS AND TREASONOUS TIPPLES

# TOFFEE APPLE SOUR

*The sky will be lit with a pyrotechnic shower, so mark the event with a Toffee Apple Sour*

Toffee apples are a staple of Bonfire Night celebrations, as apple harvests are done over the autumn period. They are the ultimate treat for a chilly evening laden with fireworks, and this Toffee Apple Sour is perfect to help make the evening complete.

**Serves** 1 • **Method** Shake • **Glassware**

### For the cocktail
*50ml apple brandy*
*30ml toffee syrup*
*20ml egg white*
*15ml lemon juice*

### For the toffee syrup
*150ml water*
*120g caster sugar*
*40g unsalted butter*
*2 tablespoons golden syrup*

To make the toffee syrup, add all the ingredients to a saucepan. Place over a medium heat, and stir constantly until it is a light golden brown colour. Remove from the heat and let cool. This makes about 180ml syrup – enough for 6 cocktails. It will keep in the fridge in a sterilised, sealed bottle or jar for up to a week, if not all used immediately. The butter may separate out from the sugar in the fridge so give it a good shake before using.

To make the cocktail, fill a cocktail shaker with ice. Add all the ingredients and shake until cold. Fine strain into an Old Fashioned glass.

### ❄ Make it a NO-ffee Apple Sour

*Substitute apple brandy for 50ml fresh granny smith apple juice and reduce the toffee syrup to 20ml.*

# BONFIRE BUTTERED RUM

*When it comes to making drinks on bonfire night, here's one to treat your friends and family right*

Bonfire night doesn't feel right without friends or family, and this buttered rum has that sentiment at its heart. This recipe was created by Dick Bradsell, drinks connoisseur and creator of the espresso martini, to serve for his family on bonfire night. Serve these buttered rum cocktails to your friends and family, and soon enough you'll have a Bonfire Night tradition of your own.

**Serves** 4 • **Method** Mix, in a large saucepan • **Glassware**

*200ml dark rum*
*200ml cloudy apple juice*
*560ml sugar syrup*
*8 dashes of Angostura bitters*
*20g unsalted butter*

**Garnish** *Freshly grated nutmeg*

Put a large saucepan over a low heat. Add all the ingredients and gently stir. Remove from the heat after 10 minutes, ladle into coffee mugs and grate over some fresh nutmeg.

# AN OL' FASHIONED CAMPFIRE

**Build your campfire right on Bonfire night**

Bonfire Night has a way of evoking all the majesty of An Ol' Fashioned Campfire – smoke, toasted marshmallows and keeping warm with good company. You won't need an actual fire in order to drink this cocktail; just a good story told well, on a night when the smell of fire lingers in the air.

Serves 1 • Method Stir • Glassware

### For the cocktail
*40ml bourbon whiskey*
*10ml (2 teaspoons) Scotch whisky*
*5ml (1 teaspoon) marshmallow syrup (see opposite)*

### For the marshmallow syrup
*25g mini marshmallows*
*125ml boiling water*
*100g caster sugar*

**Garnish** *Toasted marshmallow, ground cinnamon (optional)*

To make the marshmallow syrup, add the marshmallows and boiling water to a bowl and stir until the marshmallows have become liquid. Add the caster sugar and stir again, until all fully combined. This makes about 200ml syrup – enough for 40 cocktails. It will keep in the fridge in a sterilised, sealed bottle or jar for up to a week, if not all used immediately.

To make the cocktail, fill an Old Fashioned glass with ice. Add all the ingredients and stir. Toast a large marshmallow and rest it on the ice in the drink.

To add a crackle of fireworks, grab a lighter and a pinch of ground cinnamon. Hold the lighter in one hand above the drink and light it. With the other hand, throw the ground cinnamon through the flame and on to the drink. Importantly, you only need a pinch of cinnamon to provide the spectacular crackle; you don't want to douse the cocktail with powder (most of it will likely end up on your kitchen worktop).

# BURNT MARTINI

### *Martini in the hand, fireworks zooming by*

*Smells of smoke and sulphur are what come to mind when we think of Bonfire night. This Burnt Martini is the perfect sensory cocktail for the occasion – the navy strength gin is the connection to gunpowder and fireworks, and the whisky rinse leaves the lingering sensation of smoke.*

**Serves** 1 • **Method** Stir • **Glassware**

*5ml (1 teaspoon) smoky scotch whisky, to rinse the glass (I used Laphroaig)*
*60ml navy strength gin*
*15ml dry vermouth*

Pour the scotch whisky into a martini glass and swirl it around to rinse the glass before tipping out any excess.

Fill a mixing glass with ice and add the gin and vermouth. Stir until chilled, then fine strain into the prepared martini glass.

If you're a fan of the big, smoky flavours, you could add the 5ml (1 teaspoon) whisky to the mixing glass with the gin and vermouth, before stirring.

# GUNPOWDER AND TREASON

*Remember, remember, the 5th of November, the gunpowder, treason and plot;*
*I know of no reason why apples in season should not be combined with scotch*

Inspired by the rhyme that often accompanies Guy Fawkes Night, the cocktail is a delicious one you can serve all evening. Here the whisky is the gunpowder, pairing dangerously with the treasonous freshly juiced apples, which are in season over this period. The whisky float then adds a smoky touch, making the Gunpowder and Treason a cocktail that should never be forgot.

Serves 1 • Method Stir • Glassware

*25ml apple brandy*
*25ml scotch whisky*
*Juice of freshly juiced apples, to top*
*10ml smoky scotch whisky, to float*

**Garnish** *Cinnamon stick*

Fill a highball glass with ice and add the brandy and whisky. Top with freshly juiced apple juice, leaving enough room for the whisky float.

Very slowly pour the smoky scotch whisky on top to float. Add the cinnamon stick to the drink to garnish.

# COCKTAILS TO CHEER TO A HAPPY NEW YEAR

# JAPANESE NEW YEAR

●●●●●●●●●●●●●●●●●●●●●●●●●●●●●●●●●●●●●●●●

### *Leave your troubles behind and keep your new year in mind*

A Japanese take on the classic martini, and a classy drink for a New Year's Eve party. In Japan, years are traditionally viewed as completely separate, with each new year providing a fresh start. Consequently, parties are held with the purpose of leaving the old year's troubles behind. In Japanese, 'Happy New Year' is *akemashite omedetou.*

A traditional martini would be stirred, but the inclusion of the sake here favours a shake. You can use any gin but opting for a Japanese gin is in theme with the drink.

**Serves** 1 ● **Method** Shake ● **Glassware**

*50ml gin (I used KI NO BI Kyoto Dry)*
*50ml sake*

**Garnish** *A lemon zest twist*

Fill a cocktail shaker with ice. Add the ingredients and shake until cold, then strain into a martini glass.

Zest the glass with the lemon twist and add it to the drink.

# HAPPY NEW YEAR

• • • • • • • • • • • • • • • • • • • • • • • • • • • • • • • • • • • • •

### *Four, three, two, one, Happy New Year to everyone*

A new year celebration is the premier occasion for bubbles, so naturally a cocktail called Happy New Year will feature champagne. But this cocktail dreams bigger for the year ahead, incorporating port and cognac for a fizzy, fruity tipple. Go in for a really good champagne with this one and treat yourself to an excellent year's beginning.

**Serves** 1 • **Method** Shake • **Glassware**

*25ml tawny port*
*7.5ml (1½ teaspoons) cognac VSOP*
*25ml orange juice*
*Brut champagne, to top*

**Garnish** *Slice of orange*

Fill a cocktail shaker with ice. Add the port, cognac and orange juice and shake until cold.

Fine strain into a chilled flute glass and top with the champagne. Garnish with a slice of orange on the rim of the glass.

# FRENCH 75

● ● ● ● ● ● ● ● ● ● ● ● ● ● ● ● ● ● ● ● ● ● ● ● ● ● ● ● ● ● ● ● ●

**Fresh, clean and sophisticated, it'll make you feel alive, so cheers to a New Year with a French 75**

Named for its kick, likened to that of the French 75mm field gun in World War 1, this cocktail was first called the French 75 in the UK, is known as the 75 Cocktail in the US, and simply 'Seventy Five' in France. This is a celebratory tipple across the globe, so what better occasion to use it for than New Year's Eve, an occasion that celebrates another trip around the sun?

Serves 1 • **Method** Shake • **Glassware**

45ml gin
15ml lemon juice
7.5ml (1½ teaspoons) sugar syrup
Champagne, to top

**Garnish** Lemon zest twist

Fill a cocktail shaker with ice. Add the gin, lemon juice and sugar syrup and shake until cold. Fine strain into a chilled champagne flute.

Zest the glass with the lemon twist and sit it on the rim of the flute.

❄️ **Make it an Au Revoir 75**
Swap the gin for a non-alcoholic botanical spirit and top with a non-alcoholic fizz.

# CUPS O' HOGMANAY KINDNESS

# FLYING SCOTSMAN

*Slainte to the Scotsman, still on the line, and cheers to new year, singing Auld Lang Syne*

A drink that takes its name from one of the world's most famous steam locomotives, the Flying Scotsman certainly has the engine room to get your Hogmanay evening up to speed. The whisky and the sweet vermouth prove a deliciously lively combination – sometimes the simplest engineering is best.

Serves 1 • Method Stir • Glassware

*60ml scotch whisky*
*50ml sweet vermouth*
*15ml sugar syrup*
*2 dashes of Angostura or aromatic bitters*

**Garnish** *Orange zest twist*

Fill a mixing glass with ice. Add all the ingredients and stir. Strain into an Old Fashioned glass filled with ice.

Zest the glass with the orange twist and add it to the drink.

# ATHOLL BROSE

*Slow New Year's morning? Then here's the solution – make drinking Atholl Brose your newest resolution*

According to Scottish legend, in 1475 the Earl of Atholl quashed a Highland rebellion by filling his enemy's drinking well with oatmeal, honey and whisky. They were captured soon after, too inebriated by the mixture to put up a fight. This legendary little tipple is inspired by that victory and is the perfect drink to kick off your New Year's Day. Take heed of history, though: enjoying too many will quash even the most well-conceived resolutions.

Serves 1 • Method Shake • Glassware

*60ml scotch whisky*
*5ml (1 teaspoon) amaretto*
*45ml oat milk*
*30ml honey*
*15ml double cream*

Garnish *Freshly grated nutmeg*

Add the whisky and honey to a cocktail shaker and stir until the honey has fully combined with the liquid.

Fill the shaker with ice, then add the other ingredients and shake until cold. Fine strain into a coupe glass and grate some nutmeg over the top of the drink.

The oat milk is essential to the recipe, so if you can't get any you can make your own by soaking oats in water overnight and straining the liquid in the morning.

### ❄ *Make it an Atholl Low-se*

*Replace the whisky with a non-alcoholic aromatic or non-alcoholic grain spirit. The 5ml amaretto will contribute little to the overall ABV at such a small volume. Or you could …*

### ❄ *Make it an Atholl NO-se*

*Replace the whisky with a non-alcoholic aromatic or grain spirit and the amaretto with 2 drops of almond extract.*

# WOULD YOU BE MY VALENTINE?

# BEE MY VALENTINE

*Honey, gin and bubbly please, the thought of you makes me go weak at the knees*

The classic Bees Knees cocktail is already a great choice to brighten up your day. But this Valentine-inspired twist adds strawberries, rosewater and fizz to make this cocktail unforgettable. A perfect glass of bubbly for Valentine's day, whether you're sharing it with someone or not.

Serves 1 • **Method** Shake • **Glassware**

### For the cocktail
*50ml gin*
*20ml lemon juice*
*20ml strawberry and honey syrup (see opposite)*
*3 drops of rosewater*
*Champagne, to top*

### For the strawberry and honey syrup
*100ml water*
*100g honey*
*5 fresh strawberries, halved*

To make the strawberry and honey syrup, add all the ingredients to a small saucepan and place over a low heat. Slowly stir so that the honey combines with the water. Take off the heat and leave to infuse with the strawberries for a couple of minutes, then remove the strawberries.

This makes about 150ml syrup – enough for 10 cocktails. It will keep in the fridge in a sterilised, sealed bottle or jar for up to a week, if not all used immediately.

To make the cocktail, fill a cocktail shaker with ice. Add everything except the champagne and shake until cold. Fine strain into a champagne flute, then top with champagne.

## ❄ *Make it a Bee Sharp*
*Swap the gin for a non-alcoholic botanical spirit.*

# GOODNIGHT SWEETHEART

*Goodnight sweetheart, time for a cosmo, do-do-do-do-do*

A simple, floral take on the classic Cosmopolitan, perfect for your Valentine. Instead of garnishing the drink itself, serve with a single Valentine's rose.

Serves 1 • **Method** Shake • **Glassware**

*35ml vodka*
*50ml cranberry juice*
*15ml rose liqueur*
*10ml (2 teaspoons) lime juice*

Fill a cocktail shaker with ice. Add all the ingredients and shake until cold. Fine strain into a chilled coupe glass.

# SURE LOOKERS FOR ST PATRICK'S DAY

# SHAMROCK

*Oh the Shamrock, the green immortal Shamrock!*
*Chosen leaf of Bard and Chief, Old Erin's native*
*Shamrock!*

Fun, boozy and green – is there a more perfect tipple for a celebration of the Irish? The Shamrock might not make you any more lucky, but it's a damn tasty drink to kick off St Patrick's Day.

Serves 1 • Method Stir • Glassware

*45ml Irish whiskey*
*45ml dry vermouth*
*15ml green chartreuse*
*15ml green creme de menthe*

**Garnish** *A shamrock or mint leaf*

Fill a mixing glass with ice. Add all the ingredients and stir.

Strain into a chilled coupe glass and garnish with a shamrock or mint leaf on the rim of the glass.

# IRISH COFFEE

● ● ● ● ● ● ● ● ● ● ● ● ● ● ● ● ● ● ● ● ● ● ● ● ● ● ● ● ● ● ● ● ● ● ● ● ● ● ● ● ●

*What a sight for sore eyes, as if straight from a*
*dream, 'twas a toddy with whiskey and coffee*
*and cream*

Sometimes called a Gaelic Coffee, or by its proper Irish name
*Caife Gaelach*, the Irish Coffee is proof that sometimes the best
drinks are the simplest. It's delicious, creamy, warm, and perfect
for a colder evening.

Maybe it's just the association with the name, but an Irish Coffee
always seems to always go best with Irish whiskey.

**Serves** 1  ●  **Method** Stir  ●  **Glassware**

*30ml double cream*
*60ml Irish whiskey*
*10ml (2 teaspoons) demerara/brown sugar syrup*
*60ml hot filtered coffee*

**Garnish** *Freshly grated nutmeg*

Add the double cream to a bowl and whip until you can't see
bubbles but be careful not to make it too thick – it still needs to be
able to pour. (You might need to add more than 30ml to the bowl
to get a volume you can whip well.) Set the cream aside.

Warm a toddy glass and add the whiskey and the sugar syrup.
Pour in the hot coffee (if you're using instant coffee you might want

to wait for it to cool a little first) and stir briefly. Float the cream on top by placing a spoon just above the liquid, bowl facing up, and slowly pour the cream on to the spoon so that it trickles onto the coffee. Grate fresh nutmeg over the top of the drink.

## ❄ *Make it a Before Midday Irish Coffee*

*Removing the whiskey is the most common way to make this a non-alcoholic drink. Otherwise, you can replace the whiskey with a non-alcoholic aromatic or non-alcoholic grain spirit.*

# INDEX

• • • • • • • • • • • • • • • • • • • • • • • • • • • • • • • •

Cocktails with an asterisk have a low-alcohol or no-alcohol alternative

# ACKNOWLEDGEMENTS

Georgia Billing, bar manager at City of London Distillery, for sloe gin inspiration

Bea Bradsell, DrinkUp.London, for an excellent recipe and an even better anecdote

Pete Clucas, head vampire, Lost Boys Pizza, for his love of all things festive

Harry Gerakis, co-director of Wet & Dry bar consultancy, for clarifying what Metaxa is

Stuart Lee, who somehow enjoys Christmas cocktails in the middle of spring

Andrea Montague, whisky expert, for her encyclopaedic knowledge on all things whisky

Gergo Murath, rum expert, for his worldly advice on all things rum

ACKNOWLEDGEMENTS

# SPECIAL THANKS

• • • • • • • • • • • • • • • • • • • • • • • • • • • • • • • • • • • • • •

Thanks to the following sources for inspiring me:

P13 *The Little Donkey* written by Eric Boswell and published 1959, P22 *We Wish You a Merry Christmas* published 1935, P25 *It's Beginning to Look a Lot like Christmas* released 1951, P27 *Rudolf the Red-nosed Reindeer* written by Johnny Marks and originally released 1949, P31 and 68 *White Christmas* written by Irving Berlina and first released by Bing Crosby in 1942, Viii and P38 *The Night Before Christmas* written by Clement Clark and first published 1823, P40 *Build Me Up Buttercup* written by Mike d'Abo and Tony Macaulay and released by the Foundations in 1968, P42 *Jolly Old Saint Nicholas* poem attributed to Emily Huntingdon Miller and song to Benjamin Hanby 1881, P44 *The Gingerbread Man* originally published 1875, P45 *Jingle Bell Rock* by Bobby Helms released 1957, P49 *The Teddy Bears' Picnic* lyrics by Jimmy Kennedy 1932, P65 *Deck the Halls* English-language lyrics written by Thomas Oliphant 1862, P69 *All I Want For Christmas is You* co-written by Mariah Carey and Walter Afanasieff and released in 1994, P72 *Santa Claus is Comin' to Town* written by J. Fred Coots and Haven Gillespie first recorded by Harry Reser and his band in 1934, P80 *The Little Drummer Boy* written by Katherine Kennicott Davis 1941 first recorded in 1951 by the Trapp Family Singers, P89 *Winter Wonderland* written in 1934 by Felix Bernard and Richard Bernard Smith first recorded by Richard Himber, P101 *Zombie* by The Cranberries released 1994, P115 *Smoke on the Water* by Deep Purple released 1972, P131 *Goodnight Sweetheart* by The Spaniels released 1954, P133 *Oh the Shamrock!* By Thomas More.

Published in 2020 by Pop Press an imprint of Ebury Publishing,
20 Vauxhall Bridge Road,
London SW1V 2SA

Pop Press is part of the Penguin Random House group of companies whose
addresses can be found at global.penguinrandomhouse.com

Emma Stokes has asserted her right to be identified as the author of this Work
in accordance with the Copyright, Designs and Patents Act 1988

First published by Pop Press in 2020

www.penguin.co.uk

A CIP catalogue record for this book is available from the British Library

ISBN 9781529107487

Illustrations: Joanne Humphrey
Text design: seagulls.net

Typeset in India by Integra Software Services Pvt. Ltd
Printed and bound in Great Britain by Clays Ltd, Elcograf S.p.A.